DRAWING MADE EASY 4 NATURE

Felix Lorenzi

Bay Books
Sydney and London

The *Drawing Made Easy* series

Volume 1, Animals
Volume 2, People
Volume 3, Perspective
Volume 4, Nature

This edition © 1984, Bay Books Pty Ltd, Sydney and London
Publisher George Barber
ISBN 0 85835 757 7

© 1979 Copypress Verlag, Armand Piatti, CH-8035, Zurich, Switzerland

Preface

In this, the fourth volume of the *Drawing Made Easy* series, nature is the subject of discussion. However, nature's variations and subtleties are infinite and it is possible to review only a relatively small number of situations. Furthermore, previous volumes have already studied some specific aspects: in Volume 1, animals; in Volume 2, people; and, in Volume 3, perspective.

This volume deals more specifically with nature: trees, flowers and different types of scenery. Once again the question arises: 'Where do I start?' This book will provide both the beginner and the more advanced sketcher with ideas and suggestions for solving the problem.

But it is not enough merely to follow instructions. Observing nature plays a vital role in learning how to draw: it improves your understanding of the object you are trying to draw. As already mentioned in the previous volumes, learning to draw means learning to look, and vice versa.

With time, everyone will discover the things he or she particularly enjoys drawing. For some it will be flowers, for others it will be landscapes, while others will be attracted by still-life drawings.

Another important addition to the instructions is imagination. It is the counterpart of reality, and reality and imagination are the primary elements of creativity.

Time and time again the beginner of any age will, when sitting in front of a blank piece of paper, feel a great insecurity. Why? Presumably he is afraid of making mistakes and spoiling his picture by drawing in the wrong line or the wrong proportions. But this worry is unjustified because it is always possible to rub out a mistake with an eraser.

It is best to start off feeling fresh and bright: the more you enjoy drawing, the better your work will be. If you begin to feel unsure of yourself, it is time to take a break or to get a new sheet of paper and find some new ideas.

Above all, have fun! Proceed step by step and just follow the instructions next to the drawings.

nstructions

'he instructions are divided into three
)arts:
tructure;
nree-dimensional drawing;
)icture composition.
)f course, it is not possible to treat
hese three areas exhaustively but
'our initiative and enthusiasm will
!nable you to vary or extend the
:oncepts introduced here. By
!xperimenting with shapes you can
liscover new ways of drawing objects
ind this is an important aspect of art.
Jot every sketch will be satisfactory,
)ut it may contain elements which in
mother drawing could be more
!ffective. And there is always one
drawing you do that will have been
worth all the effort!

_et us examine each of the three
!lements individually.

Structure

Vhat is meant by 'structure'? In the
artistic sense, it refers to the
appearance of a particular surface. For
nstance, you are standing in front of a
tree, looking at the leaves. You can
more or less make out the individual
leaves — you can see the outer ones
completely but those underneath are
partly covered. In this way you get an
mage of the leaves although you
never see the actual shape of each
eaf. This particular appearance is
:alled structure. Move away from the
tree a little and look at the leaves from
a distance. Now it is no longer possible
to see the outline of the individual
leaves. Rather, you see them as a
single form. This is a structure, too,
albeit quite different from the previous
one. The structure is finer — individual
details can no longer be seen; instead
you see large groups of leaves in their
entirety. The same thing applies to a
fur coat, a woollen jumper, wire
netting, a cliff or a field. If you look at
all these surfaces close up, you can
see almost all the details. If you look at
them from some distance, then it is an
overall structure that you see.

When drawing, your task is to depict
these structures in such a way that
someone else can recognise them. It
would be inaccurate to draw every leaf
of a tree, or every single blade of grass
in a field. Instead, you must find a
structure which best approximates
what you see.

Three-dimensional drawing

Here the methods introduced in the
previous three volumes come into
play. For instance, when drawing a
leaf it is necessary to establish its
basic geometric shape. Leaves can be
many different sizes and shapes.
Simple strips of paper are a help: for a
long, thin leaf, just cut off a long, thin
strip; if the leaf is rounder, cut out a
circle. Then draw the actual shapes of

the leaves on these pieces of paper. Let them hang over the edge of the table and watch them begin to bend — you can copy them and so produce a three-dimensional picture. You will also be able to see clearly which side is actually visible: first the upper side and then the lower side (see pages 28 and 31).

Remember that trees, or groups of trees, have three dimensions. And they have a basic geometric shape as well. Shading can be a great help here.

A third point concerns landscapes. In order to draw an imaginative landscape you could try taking a piece of white cloth; wrinkle it up a bit if the landscape is to be hilly. Thus you can see how light and shadow fall and try to draw it (see page 23).

The composition of the picture

This is a difficult subject. Above all, it concerns the question of how an object stands in relation to the drawing as a whole. Every object has a particular shape and you should try to place it in your drawing in a pleasing and effective way. if there are to be several objects in the picture then these together will form a particular shape. This overall shape must be seen in relation to the actual format of the paper. This relationship can be interesting, or it can be boring or messy. Contrasting shapes help to produce an interesting composition. For instance, if a particular landscape contains predominantly round trees and bushes, you could add interest by drawing in other types of shapes as well — perhaps tall, narrow poplars or firs. Conversely, if the drawing contains mainly narrow, long shapes, you might include some horizontal shapes to provide contrast (see pages 41, 42 and 43).

Another important aspect is the format of the picture itself. You can have a square, rectangular (vertical or horizontal), triangular, or round (circular or elliptical) format. It is vital that you choose the appropriate format for your particular drawing. Beginners usually tend to ignore this point, but it is really very important. To understand better the matter of format, observe the works of the great masters.

Finally, a more general comment: drawing should always be enjoyable. As soon as you feel that you are forcing yourself to continue you should take a break and only resume when you really want to.

The examples in this book can be easily photocopied, so you can complete them with a pencil. By copying the structures your confidence will be increased.

Now, carry on with the work, and let your imagination guide you. You will soon discover an exciting and relaxing new hobby!

A beginner who wants to draw a tree knows how difficult it can be. Normally he will produce something which looks like the drawing at left. Of course, this is far from satisfactory — perhaps it would help to draw the leaves a little more precisely.

The second picture is not particularly good either. The proportions of the leaves and the trunk are incorrect. That problem can be rectified by making the trunk narrower. However, there remains the problem of how to draw the leaves. Of course, each individual leaf cannot be drawn, so what can be done? You could resort to a rather uncontrolled pattern, as in the third picture. But these leaves look more like a messily rolled-up ball of wool than anything else. The fourth picture comes closer to the desired effect.

But what makes this picture different from the others? The trunk has become much narrower and now has a definite structure, similar to that of bark. The leaves have a more orderly pattern, which makes them look more like real leaves.

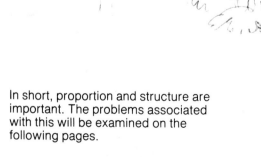

In short, proportion and structure are important. The problems associated with this will be examined on the following pages.

narrow garden fence

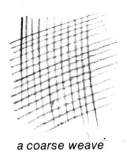

a coarse weave

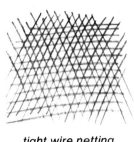

tight wire netting

shaggy fir

knitted woollen surface

tiled roof

bush with narrow leaves

large, jagged leaves

stony surface

Every object has a particular surface, which can be depicted by the use of different artistic structures. These drawings provide some examples.

Start with simple layers of lines. If line after line is drawn in a certain effect will be achieved. Or the lines can be criss-crossed to produce something like wire netting.

The lines can also be curved, in which case a bush with rounded leaves will be the result. The structures shown above can be used for all sorts of objects.

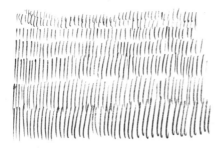

You can draw a lawn using the simple 'line-by-line' method. If structures are combined, different sorts of surfaces can be created: lawns with flower elements, large-leafed or fine, jagged-leafed plants, or wild fields. Look for new combinations.

Here are some examples of different
structural combinations: stones and
plants, wood and leaves (coarsely and
finely jagged).

These drawings show
different bushes. Look closely
at the particular types of
structures used.

Here are some examples of conifers. The drawing above on the right uses the same structure as a fur coat and is therefore not suitable for conifers. Below, the example is a branch from a pine tree. Look closely at the bark.

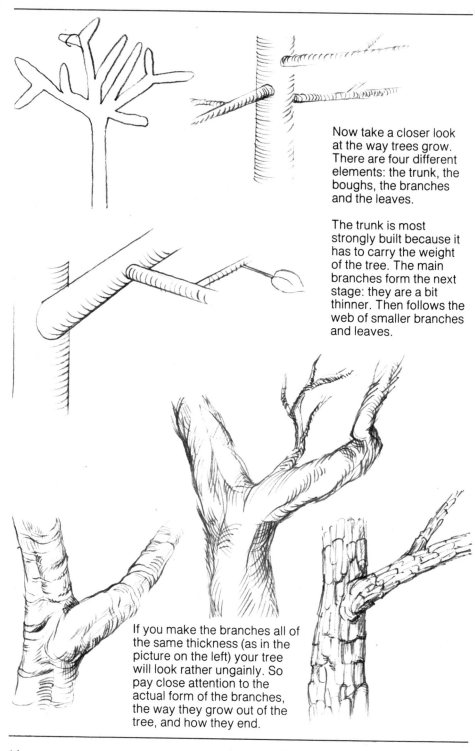

Now take a closer look at the way trees grow. There are four different elements: the trunk, the boughs, the branches and the leaves.

The trunk is most strongly built because it has to carry the weight of the tree. The main branches form the next stage: they are a bit thinner. Then follows the web of smaller branches and leaves.

If you make the branches all of the same thickness (as in the picture on the left) your tree will look rather ungainly. So pay close attention to the actual form of the branches, the way they grow out of the tree, and how they end.

These different bark types
have been made up, yet they
still look as though they
belong to real trees.

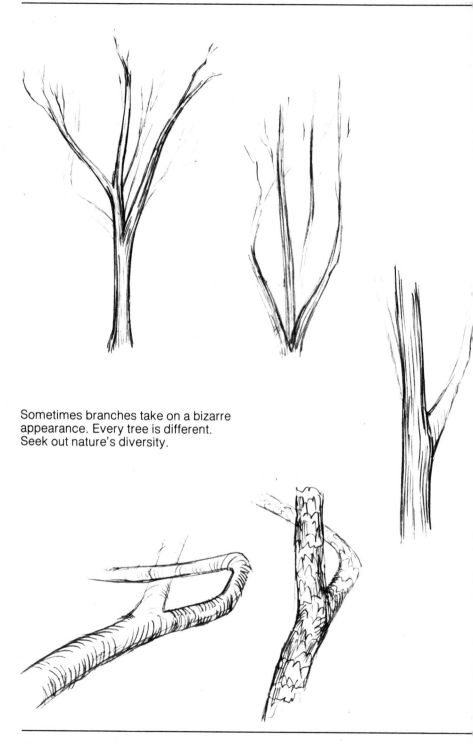

Sometimes branches take on a bizarre
appearance. Every tree is different.
Seek out nature's diversity.

Here you see leaves and bark in combination. The typical shapes of trees gradually become more significant. Each type has a definite and unmistakable appearance.

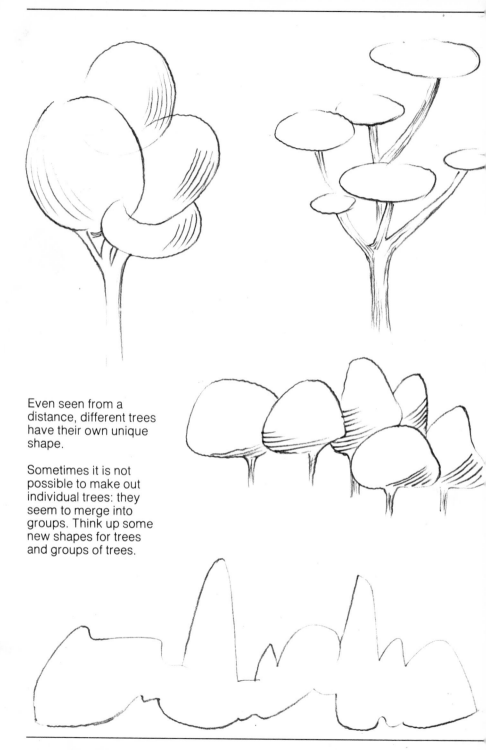

Even seen from a distance, different trees have their own unique shape.

Sometimes it is not possible to make out individual trees: they seem to merge into groups. Think up some new shapes for trees and groups of trees.

Examples of different shapes.

The typical shapes of
some well-known trees:
a spruce, a pine, a
willow and an apple tree.

These examples show combinations of various shapes. This is the first drawing of a landscape.

Note the relationship between the sizes of the trees and the people.

First attempts at landscape drawing. A few wavy lines in the background will give the impression of a hilly landscape. Then you can distribute trees and bushes as you wish. Notice how each picture has its own character.

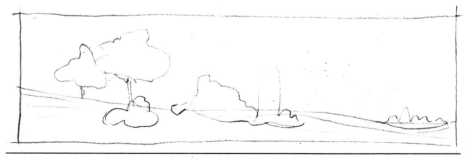

There is one very simple way of drawing imaginative landscapes: take a white cloth, wrinkle it up a little, and just draw the folds as you see them, using curved lines. Then you can add the trees of your choice.

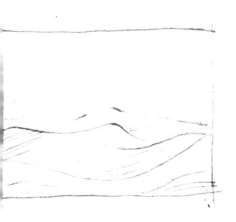

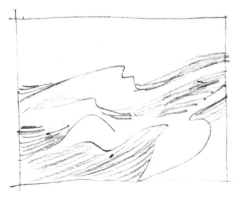

Here are a few examples of what you can do by using only lines. Let your pencil glide freely over the paper and it will produce almost by itself some very interesting structures.
Left: reflections on water.
Right: broken ice.

A large-leafed hedge.

A field covered in flowers

Use your pencil freely. In this way you can create amazing patterns. The top two look like the grain of wood, the ones in the centre resemble splinters of glass.

Below: broad landscapes are easy to draw.

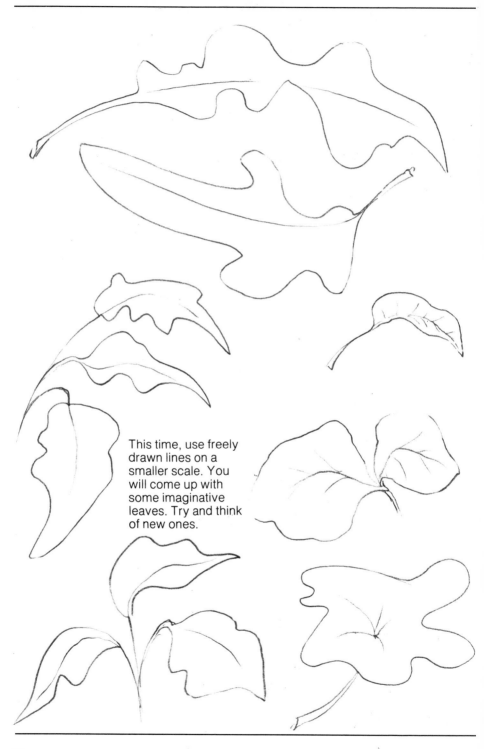

This time, use freely
drawn lines on a
smaller scale. You
will come up with
some imaginative
leaves. Try and think
of new ones.

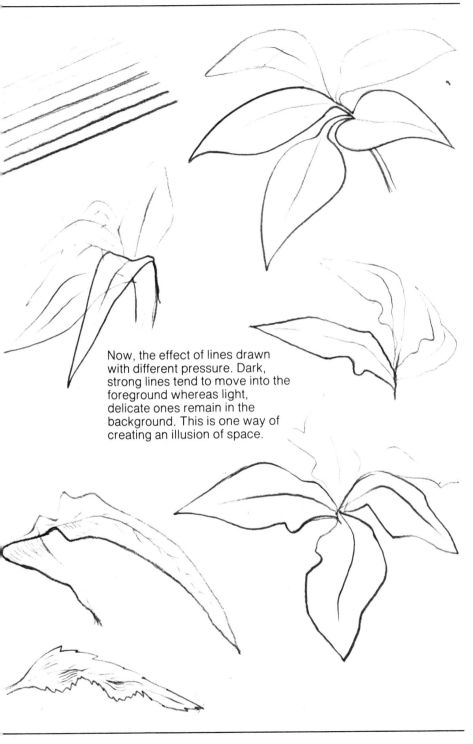

Now, the effect of lines drawn
with different pressure. Dark,
strong lines tend to move into the
foreground whereas light,
delicate ones remain in the
background. This is one way of
creating an illusion of space.

Now try to work out how to draw leaves, flowers and fruit in three dimensions. Rolled-up strips of paper are a useful aid in perspective drawing. With them, you can see clearly how the sides of the leaf become visible. Then, with fine lines, you can copy what you see.

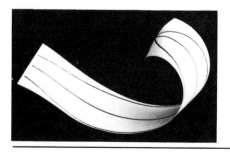

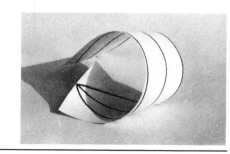

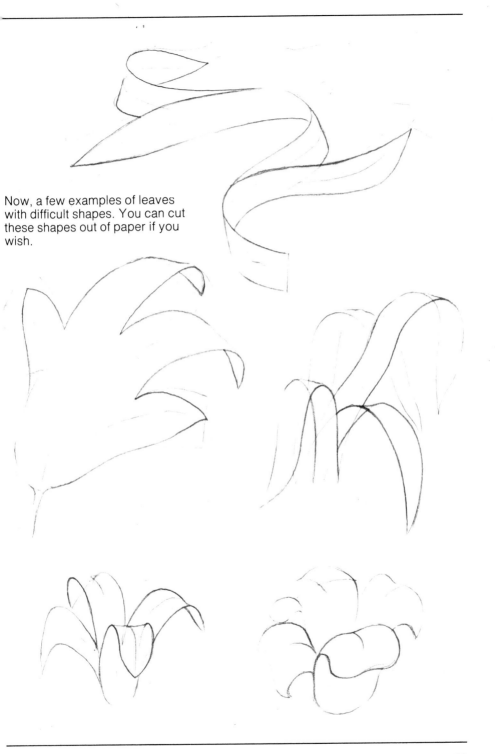

Now, a few examples of leaves with difficult shapes. You can cut these shapes out of paper if you wish.

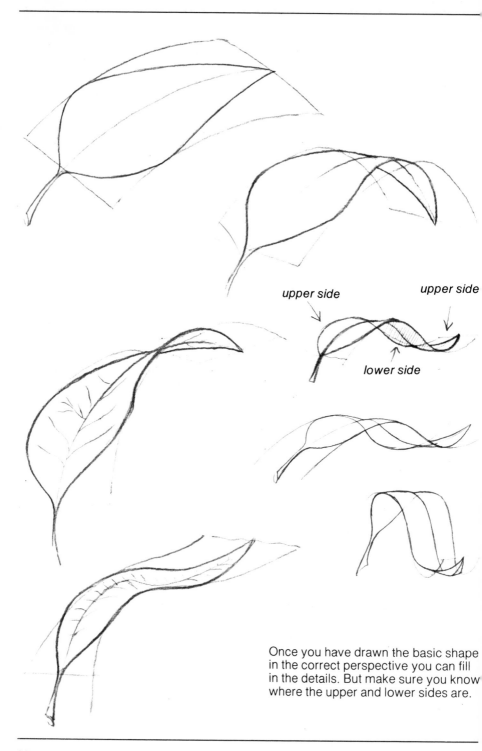

upper side

upper side

lower side

Once you have drawn the basic shape
in the correct perspective you can fill
in the details. But make sure you know
where the upper and lower sides are.

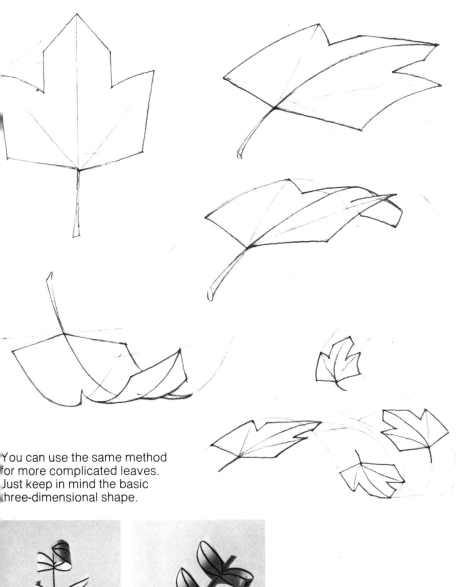

You can use the same method for more complicated leaves. Just keep in mind the basic three-dimensional shape.

Examples of how you can cut the shapes out of paper.

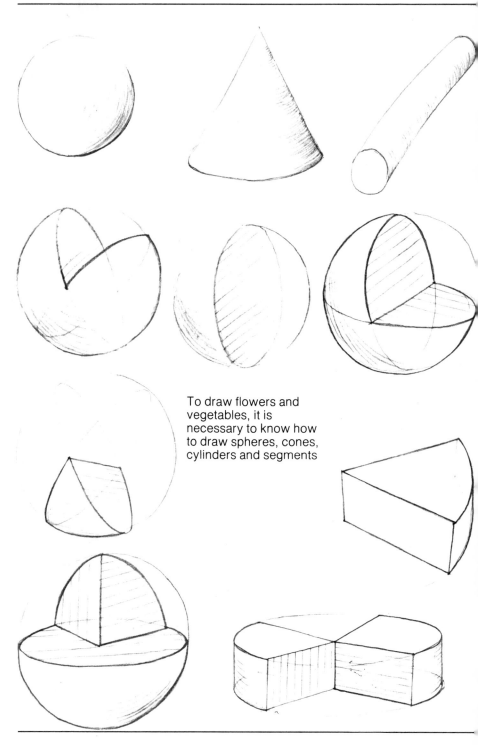

To draw flowers and vegetables, it is necessary to know how to draw spheres, cones, cylinders and segments

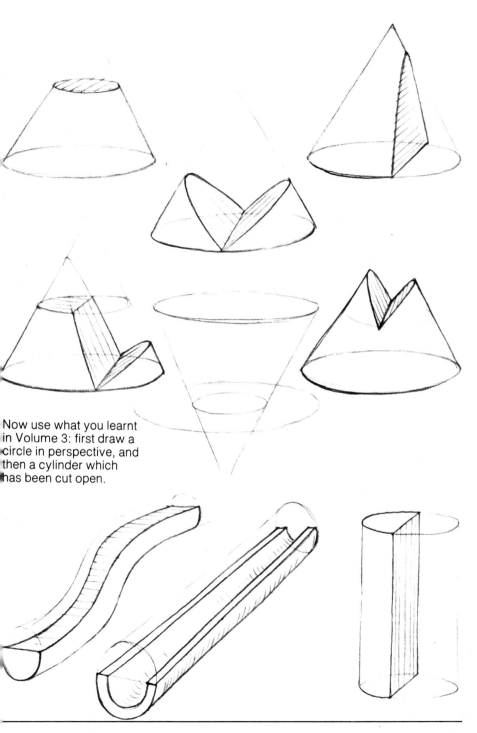

Now use what you learnt
in Volume 3: first draw a
circle in perspective, and
then a cylinder which
has been cut open.

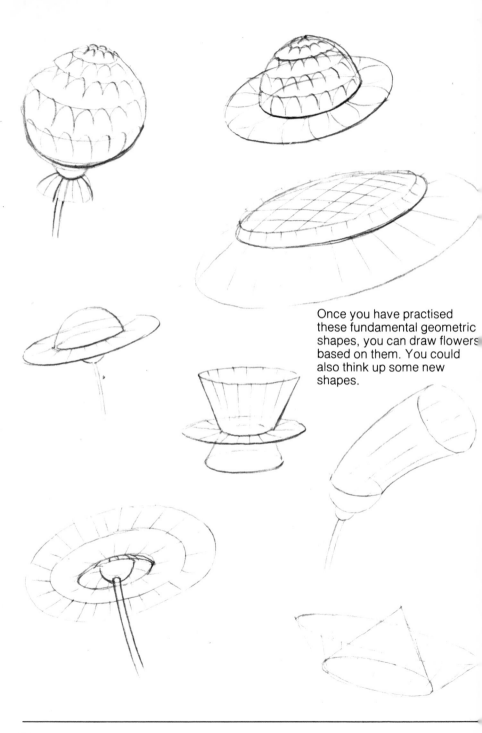

Once you have practised these fundamental geometric shapes, you can draw flowers based on them. You could also think up some new shapes.

You are able to draw more complex
shapes, too. Use strips of paper.

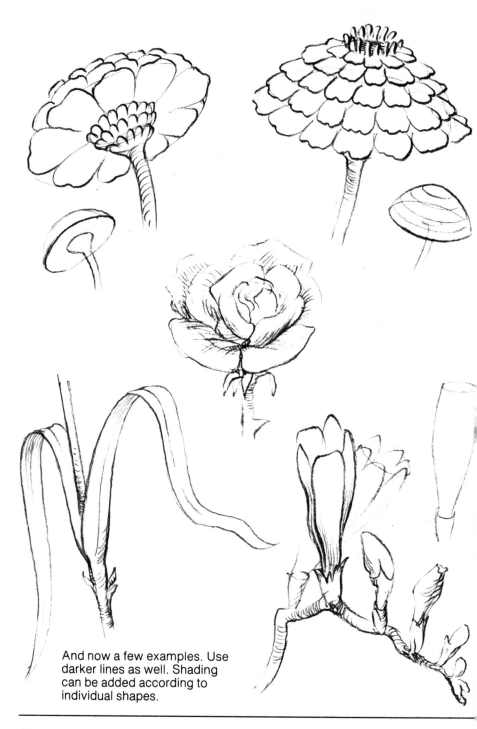

And now a few examples. Use
darker lines as well. Shading
can be added according to
individual shapes.

Think about how the basic shapes of
leaves and flowers appear, and then
how certain parts cover others.

Now for a look at fruit and vegetables. Try to find their basic three-dimensional shapes.

You could use these examples in a
still-life drawing. It is just a matter of
arranging them in an interesting
fashion.

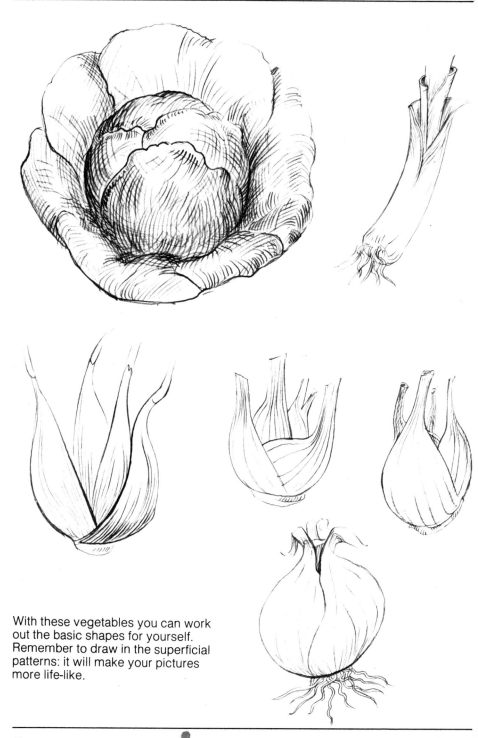

With these vegetables you can work out the basic shapes for yourself. Remember to draw in the superficial patterns: it will make your pictures more life-like.

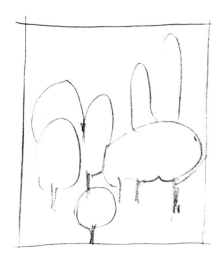

Finally, a word about the composition of your picture. The most important consideration is how objects should be placed in relation to the dimensions of the sheet of paper. There are boring compositions and interesting ones, and the mark of a good composition is that it contains contrasting shapes: large and small, long and short, pointed and round, straight and curved, full and empty, thick and thin, and so on. These contrasts help to create an interesting picture, but they must suit the dimensions of the paper used.

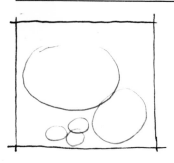

Here are only round shapes, but they do vary in size. This provides the contrast of small and large.

Long shapes: a contrast of long and short, and also of thick and thin.

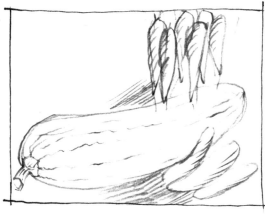

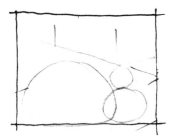

Round and straight shapes: a contrast of round and straight, and also of large and small.

large — small

round — pointed

long — short

horizontal — vertical

tranquil — cluttered

curved — straight

The position of the objects on your piece of paper is very important. Look for further contrasts.

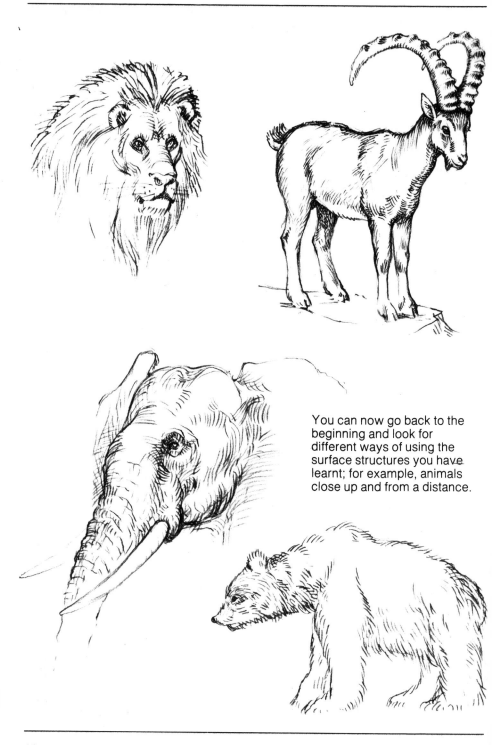

You can now go back to the
beginning and look for
different ways of using the
surface structures you have
learnt; for example, animals
close up and from a distance.

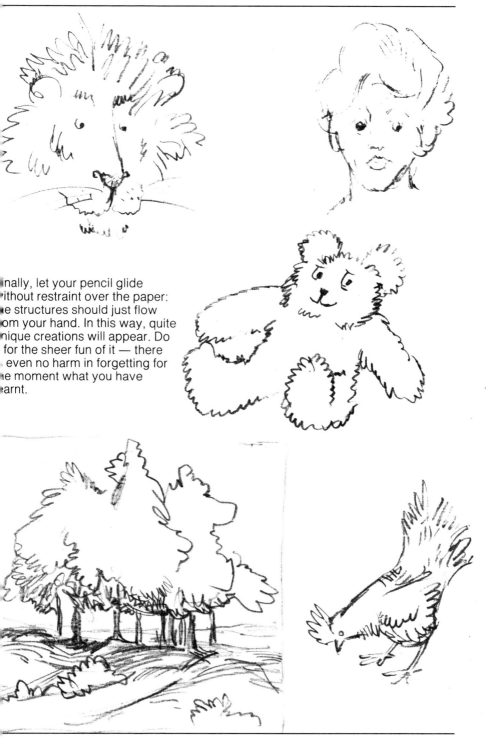

nally, let your pencil glide
ithout restraint over the paper:
e structures should just flow
om your hand. In this way, quite
nique creations will appear. Do
for the sheer fun of it — there
even no harm in forgetting for
e moment what you have
arnt.

Conclusion

Drawing should not be left to the highly talented. It is a matter of learning to see, and understanding what you have seen. Perhaps this little tour through nature has given you enough encouragement to get to know better the various shapes in nature and to try and draw them.

Printed in Singapore